# Hey Diddle-Diddle
# तुन-तुन तरा-तरा

D1822742

*मेरी प्यारी*
*जुजु और गुगु*
*के लिए*

**बाबली मोइत्रा सराफ़**

वाणी प्रकाशन

वाणी प्रकाशन

4695, 21-ए, दरियागंज, नयी दिल्ली 110 002

*शाखा*

*अशोक राजपथ, पटना 800 004*

फ़ोन : +91 11 23273167 फ़ैक्स : +91 11 23275710

www.vaniprakashan.in
vaniprakashan@gmail.com
sales@vaniprakashan.in

TUN-TUN TARA-TARA
*by* Babli Moitra Saraf
*Illustrated by* Dhawani Mahajan

ISBN : 978-93-87409-45-3
Nursery Rhymes/Poetry

© 2017 Babli Moitra Saraf

First Edition

मूल्य : ₹150

© 2017 बाबली मोइत्रा सराफ़

चित्रांकन : ध्वनि महाजन

इस पुस्तक के किसी भी अंश को किसी भी माध्यम में प्रयोग

करने के लिए प्रकाशक से लिखित अनुमति लेना अनिवार्य है।

*आर.टेक ऑफसेट, दिल्ली-110 032 में मुद्रित*

*Vani Prakashan's signature motif is created by Artist Maqbool Fida Husain*

*वाणी प्रकाशन का लोगो मक़बूल फ़िदा हुसेन की कूची से*

# Preface

Do we know a child who hasn't raised her little palm and flung fingers to enact 'Twinkle-twinkle little star...' or twisted her tiny waist to the tune of 'Humpty-Dumpty sat on a wall...'? Barely! Apart from being perfect first stories for our children, nursery rhymes have been among the best educational tools to teach community living, language learning, vocabulary, and for motor skills improvement and coordination. At the same time, child educationists across the world profess that it is equally imperative to enable first learning of a child in her mother tongue. This equips her with the intuitive cognition needed to develop linguistic structures, grammar and syntax. In the globalised world we inhabit, these faculties are necessary for holistic, inclusive upbringing and multi-lingual capabilities.

These two thoughts are the building blocks for this beautiful book you hold in your hands. It brings us immense pleasure to present you a collection of Hindi translations and adaptations of popular nursery rhymes originally written in English. Linguist, educationist and translator Dr. Babli Moitra Saraf shares, "the verses grew spontaneously out of playing with the English rhymes with my daughters when they were small and it was like a game. The rhymes succeeded for me when the girls responded joyfully to them and contributed their own two bits. They are actually adaptations rather than translations. The language and cultural setting change, but the basic rhyme structure and metre are sought to be maintained along with a general sense of the original verse. The vocabulary and the register is colloquial and appropriate to a child's world. Yet other worlds open up through them. Some basic grammar, vocabulary and punctuation is intended in the written text but the rhymes can as well be recited aloud to a beat and melody. An audio version may a well be the next step".

It takes a master to bridge the distance between the English rhyme and Hindi *chhand*, baseball and cricket, a pine tree and a *peepal* tree, between the portrait of Shakespeare and that of Tagore... between the ambiguous sense of foreign sensibility and a child's immediate culturally enriched 'non-sense' that is much celebrated by pioneers like Sukumar Ray. Dr. Moitra Saraf has accomplished this with love and a smile that will be contagious as you flip the following pages.

'Anuwad' is the essence of life-it is born out of confluence of ideas waiting to take shape in the hearts and minds of those who engage with them. The ideas are expressed, and not limited, by media. They flow seamlessly through words, paintings, music and performative art forms. This is the core concept behind this production that has been decorated with culturally sensitive illustrations by Dhawani Mahajan. The bridge that Dr. Moitra Saraf creates is brought to an Indian life through the *jugalbandi* of these two fascinating artists.

**-Aditi Maheshwari-Goyal**

***Publisher***

# Contents


| | |
|---|---|
| Jack and Jill | 6 |
| My Red Balloon | 8 |
| Old Mother Hubbard | 10 |
| Rain, Rain, Go Away | 12 |
| Hickory-Dickory-Dock | 14 |
| Twinkle-Twinkle Little Star | 16 |
| Little Boy Blue | 18 |
| The Itsy-Bitsy Spider | 20 |
| Pussy Cat, Pussy Cat | 22 |
| Humpty Dumpty Sat on a Wall | 24 |
| Mary Had a Little Lamb | 26 |
| Little Bo-Peep | 28 |
| Hey Diddle-Diddle | 30 |
| Simple Simon Met a Pieman | 32 |
| Hush, Little Baby | 34 |

# अनुक्रम


| | |
|---|---|
| छोटी छोटा | 7 |
| लाल गुब्बारा | 9 |
| बूढ़ी नानी समझ न पाए | 11 |
| बरखा रानी, बरखा रानी | 13 |
| घड़ी बोली टक–टक | 15 |
| टिम–टिम तारा | 17 |
| मुन्ने राजा आओ | 19 |
| छोटी–सी मकड़ी | 21 |
| बिल्ली मौसी, बिल्ली मौसी | 23 |
| दीवार पे बैठा अंडा बाबा | 25 |
| मिनि की बकरी | 27 |
| मिनि की बकरी चलते–चलते | 29 |
| तुन–तुन तरा–तरा | 31 |
| भोले भाई को मिला हलवाई | 33 |
| चुप मेरी मुन्नी अब न रो | 35 |

Jack and Jill
Went up the hill,
To fetch a pail of water.
Jack fell down,
And broke his crown,
And Jill came tumbling after.

छोटी छोटा
उठा के लोटा,
चले हैं देखो पानी भरने।
फिसला छोटा,
लुढ़का लोटा,
छोटी भागी उसे पकड़ने।

My red balloon,
My red balloon,
Flies high, flies high, flies high!
I jumped up high
To catch it fly
But could not reach it, why?

लाल गुब्बारा
प्यारा-प्यारा
ऊँचा यूँ लहराया है।
हम झपटे हैं उसे पकड़ने
फिर क्यूँ हाथ न आया है?

Old Mother Hubbard,
Went to the cupboard,
To get her poor dog a bone.
But when she got there,
The cupboard was bare,
And so the poor dog
had none.

बूढ़ी नानी समझ न पाए
उसका कुत्ता अब क्या खाए?
कुत्ता भूखा, बर्तन सूखा,
नानी रोई हाय-हाय!

Rain, rain, go away
Come again another day!
Rain, rain, go away
Little Johnny wants to play!

बरखा रानी, बरखा रानी,
और न तुम बरसाओ पानी!
पलट के आना फिर कभी,
मुन्ना चाहे खेलूँ अभी।

Hickory-dickory-dock,
The mouse ran up the clock!
The clock struck one!
Down the mouse ran!
Hickory-dickory-dock.

घड़ी बोली टक-टक,
चूहा चढ़ गया झटपट!
घड़ी बोली डंग-डंग,
चूहा भागा एक दम!

Twinkle-twinkle little star,
How I wonder what you are.
Up above the world so high,
Like a diamond in the sky!

टिम-टिम तारा,
कितना न्यारा।
दूर गगन में,
अपनी धुन में
सदा चमकता रहता तू।
हीरे जैसा लगता तू!

Little Boy Blue,
Come blow up your horn!
The sheep's in the meadow,
The cow's in the corn!
Where is the boy,
Who looks after the sheep?
He's in the haystack,
Fast asleep.

मुन्ने राजा आओ,
बाजा तो बजाओ।
गाय गई खेत में,
बकरी गई रेत में।
मुन्ना राजा कहाँ गया?
पेड़ की छाँव में सो गया!

The itsy-bitsy spider
Climbed up the waterspout.
Down came the rain,
And washed the spider out.
Out came the sun,
And dried up all the rain.
So the itsy-bitsy spider
Climbed up the spout again!

छोटी-सी मकड़ी,
घर से निकली।
पानी जो बरसा,
हो गई गीली।
सूरज चमका,
मकड़ी मचली।
फिर देखो वो,
घर से निकली।

Pussy cat, Pussy cat,
Where have you been?
"I've been to London
To look at the Queen."

Pussy cat, Pussy cat,
What did you do there?
"I frightened a little mouse
Under the chair."

बिल्ली मौसी, बिल्ली मौसी
कहाँ गई थी?
"जयपुर में रहती है रानी
मिलने गई थी।"
बिल्ली मौसी, बिल्ली मौसी
तुमने वहाँ क्या-क्या किया?
"कुर्सी के नीचे था चूहा
उसको मैंने डरा दिया!"

Humpty Dumpty
Sat on a wall,
Humpty Dumpty
Had a great fall!
All the king's horses,
And all the king's men,
Could not put Humpty
Together again

दीवार पे बैठा अंडा बाबा,
ओ-हो गिर गया अंडा बाबा!
सारे लोग गए हैं डर,
अब कौन जोड़े उसका सर?

Mary had a little lamb,
Its fleece was white as snow
And everywhere that Mary went,
The lamb was sure to go.
It followed her to school one day,
Which was against the rule,
It made the children laugh and play,
To see a lamb at school!

मिनि की बकरी,
संग-संग निकली।
जहाँ भी वो जाए,
पीछे-पीछे आए।
चलते-चलते पहुँची स्कूल,
मिनि से देखो हो गई भूल।
बच्चों ने तो लिया मज़ा,
मिनि बेचारी को मिली सज़ा।

Little Bo-Peep
Has lost her sheep.
And doesn't know where
To find them.
Leave them alone,
And they'll come home,
Carrying their tails
Behind them.

मिनि की बकरी चलते-चलते
कहाँ न जाने खोई है।
मिनि बेचारी देखो कितना,
सिसक-सिसक के रोई है।

मिनि अब तुम चुप हो जाओ,
वापस अपने घर को जाओ।
शाम होते ही वो टहलती,
आ जाएगी पूँछ हिलाती।

Hey diddle-diddle,
The cat and the fiddle.
The cow jumped over the moon.
The little dog laughed,
To see such sport,
And the dish ran away with the spoon.

तुन-तुन तरा-तरा,
बिल्ला बजाये इकतारा।
गाय ने जो मारी छलाँग,
देखो पार कर गई चाँद!
देख पिल्ला खिल-खिलाया,
खेल ये उसको कैसा भाया!
मौज, मस्ती, रंग-उमंग,
थाली भागी चमचे संग!

Simple Simon met a pieman,
Going to the fair.
Said Simple Simon to the pieman,
"Let me taste your ware."
Said the pieman to Simple Simon,
"Show me first your penny."
Said Simple Simon to the pieman,
"Indeed, I have not any!"

भोले भाई को मिला हलवाई
मेले में जाते हुए ।
कहे भोले भाई, "चखें रसमलाई,
संग-संग चलते हुए?"
कहे हलवाई, "ओ भोले भाई,
पैसे तो हैं न साथ?"
कहे भोले भाई, "पास न पाई,
निकला हूँ मैं खाली हाथ!"

Hush, little baby, don't say a word,
Papa's gonna buy you a mockingbird.

And if that mockingbird won't sing,
Papa's gonna buy you a diamond ring.

And if that diamond ring turns brass,
Papa's gonna buy you a looking glass.

And if that looking glass is cracked,
Papa's gonna buy you a horse and cart.

And if that horse and cart fall down?
You'll still be the prettiest girl in town!

चुप मेरी मुन्नी अब न रो
पापा ले आएँगे तोते दो।
गर वो तोते न बोले तो,
पापा लेके आएँगे टॉफी दो।
गर वो टॉफी तू खा ले तो,
पापा ले के आएँगे पिल्ले दो।

गर वो पिल्ले न भौंके तो,
पापा ले आएँगे टमटम को।
और जो घोड़े रुक जाएँ तो...?
फिर भी तुम परियों की रानी हो!

**Babli Moitra Saraf** is the Principal of Indraprastha College for Women, University of Delhi and an Associate Professor in its Department of English and Head of the Department of Multi Media and Mass Communication. She has received her M.Phil degree in English and PhD in Sociology. Her teaching interests include Modern Indian Literature in Translation, Classical Literature, Renaissance and Modern European Drama, Poetry, Cultural Studies, Communication Studies, Literary Theory, Literature and the Arts and the Hindi Film Song. She is fluent in several Indian and foreign languages.

Her publications, *La Cattura* (Theoria, 1996) and *La Preda e altri Racconti* (Einaudi, 2004), are translations from the Bengali activist-novelist Mahasweta Devi's works into Italian in collaboration with Maria Federica Oddera. Her work *Rajouri Remembered* (2007), is a translation of a family narrative, from Hindi, Urdu and oral Punjabi, which recounts the effects of the Partition of India in the state of Jammu and Kashmir. She has published articles in the field of Translating and Interpreting Studies. Her latest publication, co-edited with Shormishtha Panja is *Performing Shakespeare in India: Exploring Indianness, Literatures and Cultures.* (New Delhi: Sage, 2016). Her ongoing research concerns Orality, Embodied Languages and Translation.

She is on the editorial board of *Translation*: a transdisciplinary journal (Rome), and of Saar Sansaar (New Delhi) journal of Hindi dedicated to translations directly from foreign languages. She is a member on the Scientific Board of In Other Wor(l)ds: Project Book Series on translations from Asia and North Africa. Department of Asian and North African Studies, Ca'Foscari University, Venice, Italy.

Moitra Saraf has been a scholar under the Indo-Italian Cultural Exchange Program, a Research Associate at the NIDA School of Translation Studies (NSTS) 2009 and Visiting Faculty at NSTS 2011. She received the Distinguished Teacher Award of the University of Delhi in 2009, the Amity Women Achiever in Education Award in 2010, the 27$^{th}$ Dr. S. Radhakrishnan Memorial National Award for Teachers in 2011, the Fulbright- Nehru International Education Administrator Seminar award in 2011. She also received the "C.F. Andrews Distinguished Alumnus Award for Lifelong Pursuit of Excellence" from St. Stephens College in 2015, the "Women of the Decade in Academia", Award of the Women Economic Forum in 2017 and the Certificate of Felicitation of the International Women's Club for "Remarkable Contribution in the Field of Administration & Education for Girls"

Babli Moitra Saraf resides in Delhi with her husband Kanti and has two daughters, Aditi and Ishani.